POMERANIANS

by Susan H. Gray

Published in the United States of America by The Child's World®
1980 Lookout Drive • Mankato, MN 56003-1705
800-599-READ • www.childsworld.com

PHOTO CREDITS

© All is Sharp Photography: 23
© Bill Aron/PhotoEdit: 27
© Efi Keren/Alamy: 25
© Hulton-Deutsch Collection/Corbis: 9
© iStockphoto.com/Jennifer Daley: 17
© iStockphoto.com/Michelle Milliman: 15
© iStockphoto.com/photopix: 11
© Mark Raycroft/Minden Pictures: 13, 21, 29
© Mitsuaki Iwago/Minden Pictures: 19
© Stockdisc Classic/Alamy: cover, 1

ACKNOWLEDGMENTS

The Child's World®: Mary Berendes, Publishing Director;
Katherine Stevenson, Editor

The Design Lab: Kathleen Petelinsek, Design and Page Production

LIBRARY OF CONGRESS CATALOGING-IN-PUBLICATION DATA

Gray, Susan Heinrichs.
   Pomeranians / by Susan H. Gray.
      p. cm. — (Domestic dogs)
   Includes index.
   ISBN 978-1-59296-966-1 (library bound : alk. paper)
   1. Pomeranian dog—Juvenile literature. I. Title. II. Series.
   SF429.P8G74 2008
   636.76—dc22   2007020794

Table of Contents

NAME That DOG!

What dog is smaller than a house cat? 🐾 What dog is stronger than it looks? 🐾 What dog has the face of a fox? 🐾 What dog has been owned by many famous people? 🐾 If you said the Pomeranian (pom-uh-RAY-nee-un), you are right!

5

Big Spitz to Little Pomeranian

Pomeranians came from dogs of the spitz family. Spitzes were strong working dogs. They lived in cold areas in northern Europe. They had wonderful, thick coats. Their fluffy tails curled over their backs. These dogs pulled sleds, herded sheep, and hunted.

Some spitzes lived in a part of Europe called Pomerania. Today that area is in Germany and Poland. Pomeranian people liked spitzes that were small. They kept choosing the

The map below shows where Germany and Poland are on Earth. The map on the right shows a closer view.

England

Wales Great Britain

Denmark

Latvia

Neth.

Lithuania

Belgium

Germany

Poland

Belaru

Lux.

France

Czech

Switzerland

Slovakia

Austria

Hungary

Slovenia

Italy

Croatia

Romania

Bosnia And Herz.

Yugoslavia

Bulgaria

Macedonia

Albania

Greece

smallest dogs in each family. Over time, the Pomeranian spitzes became quite small.

People in other countries learned about these little spitzes. In 1888, Queen Victoria of England became the owner of one. She named him Marco. The queen loved little Marco. She would not let him out of her sight. People all across England heard about Marco. Soon they wanted Pomeranian dogs, too. The little dogs became **popular**. Many wealthy people owned them.

People brought some of these little dogs to the United States. In 1892, Pomeranians appeared in American dog shows. After that, more and more people wanted them. Today, Pomeranians are popular dogs in the U.S. In fact, they are the nation's fourteenth most popular **breed**.

There are still dogs called spitzes today. They are bigger than Pomeranians. They still have beautiful, thick coats.

This photo shows a woman and her Pomeranian in 1913.

Furry Little Toys

Pomeranians are small dogs. Adults are only 7 to 12 inches (18 to 30 centimeters) tall at the shoulder. They weigh 3 to 7 pounds (1 to 3 kilograms). That is half as heavy as a house cat. But Pomeranians are strong for their size.

Pomeranians' eyes are dark. Their little faces are foxlike. Their short ears stand straight up. The ears are hard to see under all that hair!

Some people say they have a "teacup" Pomeranian. This is not a different breed. It is just a very small dog.

You can see how little this Pom is next to some flowers.

11

Poms have beautiful double coats. The undercoat is close to the body. It has short, soft, thick hair. It keeps the dogs warm. The outer coat has long, shiny hair. This long hair is pretty. But it feels hard to the touch. The fur around the dog's neck is extra thick. This thick hair is called a *ruff*. The dog's tail is long and feathery. It lies down on the Pomeranian's back. When a Pom wags its tail, the long hair swishes back and forth.

Pomeranians come in different colors. They might be gold, tan, orange, reddish, cream, or bluish gray. Some Poms are a mix of colors.

Poms belong to a group of small dogs called "toy" dogs. There are many kinds of toy dogs. Chihuahuas (chih-WAH-wuz), pugs, and Yorkshire terriers are toy dogs, too.

Here you can see two different Pomeranian colors.

Little Dog, Big Spirit

Pomeranians are smart and full of energy. They love to learn tricks. They are **loyal** to their owners. They can be very bold for their size.

Mostly these are good things in a dog. But Pomeranians sometimes take things too far. They often try too hard to **protect** their owners. They bark at the doorbell. They bark at visitors. They bark at other animals. Sometimes they even attack larger dogs.

This girl loves her Pomeranian.

But Poms can learn to act differently. Good owners do not let their dogs keep barking. They teach their dogs how to behave. They gently train them to follow **commands**. Then the dogs know how to be good dogs!

It is helpful for Poms to grow up with other pets. That helps them get along with other animals. It is also good for them to be around people. Poms are great pets for older people and single people. They are fine for families with older children. Very young children can make Poms nervous and jumpy.

Pomeranians do well in small homes or apartments.

Some owners buy costumes for Poms and other toy dogs. They dress their dogs as Cinderella, Zorro, and even Spiderman!

This girl is training her Pomeranian to sit.

Pom Puppies

Most Pomeranian mothers have one to three puppies in a **litter**. The newborns weigh about as much as a lemon. They have rounded heads and tiny ears. Their eyes are tightly closed. Their ears cannot hear yet. Their legs are too weak for walking. Their tails are not strong enough to wag.

The puppies have soft, fluffy fur. But it is not enough to keep them warm. They snuggle close to their mothers and to each other. That keeps them safe and warm.

These Pom puppies are only a few weeks old.

A lot changes in the puppies' first few weeks. The pups open their eyes and start looking around. They start to hear things. They hear their brothers and sisters whining. Their legs get stronger. They begin to move around. At first they fall over a lot. But soon they can walk and run.

At three months, Poms start losing their soft puppy fur. Their coats look ragged for a while. Slowly their new coats grow in. Their round heads begin to look pointy and foxlike. Their tails start curling up over their backs. Now the dogs start to look like grown-up Poms.

Poms and other small dogs are sometimes called "lap dogs." They are small enough to curl up on someone's lap.

Here you can see a Pom puppy (right) next to an adult. The puppy is about eight weeks old.

Heroes and Lap Dogs

Many people keep Pomeranians as pets. They love these cute, smart, fearless little dogs. Some Poms have even become heroes. Ginger was a Pom who lived in New Jersey. She was very old. She could not hear. She was missing some teeth. One day, someone broke into her home. Ginger's owner was frightened. But Ginger sprang into action. She bit the stranger's ankles until he ran away! Ginger won an award for her bravery.

Ginger won a special award for saving her owner's life.

23

Most Pomeranians never become heroes like Ginger. But some win awards in dog shows. Their owners brush their long hair. They teach the dogs to behave. They enter them in shows all over the country.

Many Pomeranians work as **therapy** dogs. They visit people who are sick or lonely. They cheer people up with their cute ways.

A Pom's main job is to be a good pet. People have loved Poms for a long time. Michelangelo (my-kul-AN-juh-lo) was a great artist. He lived 500 years ago. His Pom rested on a pillow while his master painted. Mozart (MOTE-zart) and Chopin (SHOW-pan) wrote wonderful music. They both wrote music for their favorite Poms.

Many movie stars have owned Poms. Elvis Presley was a famous singer. He had a Pom named Sweet Pea.

This Pom is cheering up a sad little boy.

25

Caring for a Pomeranian

Pomeranians are known for their beautiful coats. But those coats need a lot of care! The long hair gets knotted or tangled easily. And these dogs shed a lot. They need to be brushed or washed often. Brushing gets rid of the loose hairs. A badly tangled coat might need clipping.

Like many toy dogs, Poms can get knee problems. Their kneecaps can slip out of place. This can be painful. The dogs can have trouble walking or running. **Veterinarians** can help with this problem.

This veterinarian is listening to a Pomeranian's heartbeat.

Owners should pay attention to their Poms' teeth. These dogs often have tooth problems. Some Poms do not lose their baby teeth. Their adult teeth start growing in anyway. Soon their mouths have too many teeth. A veterinarian might need to pull the baby teeth out. Some Poms have gums that are not healthy. That can make them lose their adult teeth. Some dry foods are good for Poms' teeth and gums. They keep the teeth clean. They keep the gums healthy.

Pomeranians need lots of care. But they are very loving in return. Healthy Poms can live long, happy lives. In fact, they can live for 15 years or more!

Many owners brush their dogs' teeth. They use special toothbrushes and toothpaste. Brushing keeps the dogs' teeth and gums healthy. Toothpaste for dogs comes in flavors like beef and chicken!

This Pomeranian looks almost as if she is smiling!

29

Glossary

breed (BREED) A breed is a certain type of an animal. Pomeranians are a well-known dog breed.

commands (kuh-MANDZ) Commands are orders to do certain things. Pomeranians can learn to follow commands.

litter (LIH-tur) A litter is a group of babies born to one animal at the same time. Most litters of Pomeranians have one to three puppies.

loyal (LOY-ul) To be loyal is to be true to something and stand up for it. Pomeranians are loyal to their owners.

popular (PAH-pyuh-lur) When something is popular, it is liked by lots of people. Pomeranians are popular.

protect (pruh-TEKT) To protect something is to keep it safe. Poms protect their owners and their homes.

therapy (THAYR-uh-pee) Therapy is treatment for an illness or other problem. Therapy dogs can cheer up people who are ill.

veterinarians (vet-rih-NAIR-ee-unz) Veterinarians are doctors who take care of animals. Veterinarians are often called "vets" for short.

To Find Out More

Books to Read

American Kennel Club. *The Complete Dog Book for Kids*. New York: Howell Book House, 1996.

Cawthera, Averil. *Living With a Pomeranian*. Hauppauge, NY: Barron's, 2003.

Ellman, Vikki. *Guide to Owning a Pomeranian*. Philadephia, PA: Chelsea House, 1999.

Jones, Happeth A. *The Pomeranian*. New York: Howell Book House, 1996.

Stocker, Marguerite. *Pomeranians*. Neptune City, NJ: T. F. H. Publications, 2006.

Places to Contact

American Kennel Club (AKC) Headquarters
260 Madison Ave, New York, NY 10016
Telephone: 212-696-8200

On the Web

Visit our Web site for lots of links about Pomeranians:

http://www.childsworld.com/links

Note to Parents, Teachers, and Librarians: We routinely check our Web links to make sure they're safe, active sites—so encourage your readers to check them out!

Index

About the Author

Susan H. Gray has a Master's degree in zoology. She has written more than 70 science and reference books for children. She loves to garden and play the piano. Susan lives in Cabot, Arkansas, with her husband Michael and many pets.